The Ultimate Lean and Green Cookbook

Fast, Easy to Make, Healthy Recipes to Stay Fit

GINA WILLIAMS

TABLE OF CONTENTS

SNACKS AND APPETIZERS 78

DESSERTS 84

BREAKFAST RECIPES

1. Millet Porridge

Preparation Time: 10 minutes

Cooking Time: 20 minutes

Servings: 2

Ingredients:

- Sea salt
- 1 tbsp. finely chopped coconuts
- 1/2 cup unsweetened coconut milk
- 1/2 cup rinsed and drained millet
- 1-1/2 cups alkaline water
- 3 drops liquid stevia

Directions:

1. Sauté the millet in a non-stick skillet for about 3 minutes.
2. Add salt and water then stir.
3. Let the meal boil then reduce the amount of heat.

4. Cook for 15 minutes then add the remaining ingredients. Stir.

5. Cook the meal for 4 extra minutes.

6. Serve the meal with toping of the chopped nuts.

Nutrition: Calories: 219 kcal Fat: 4.5g Carbs: 38.2g Protein: 6.4g

2. Jackfruit Vegetable Fry

Preparation Time: 5 minutes

Cooking Time: 5 minutes

Servings: 6

Ingredients:

- 2 finely chopped small onions
- 2 cups finely chopped cherry tomatoes
- 1/8 tsp. ground turmeric
- 1 tbsp. olive oil
- 2 seeded and chopped red bell peppers
- 3 cups seeded and chopped firm jackfruit
- 1/8 tsp. cayenne pepper
- 2 tbsps. chopped fresh basil leaves
- Salt

Directions:

1. In a greased skillet, sauté the onions and bell peppers for about 5 minutes.
2. Add the tomatoes then stir.
3. Cook for 2 minutes.

4. Then add the jackfruit, cayenne pepper, salt, and turmeric.

5. Cook for about 8 minutes.

6. Garnish the meal with basil leaves.

7. Serve warm.

Nutrition: Calories: 236 kcal Fat: 1.8g Carbs: 48.3g Protein: 7g

3. Zucchini Pancakes

Preparation Time: 15 minutes

Cooking Time: 8 minutes

Servings: 8

Ingredients:

- 12 tbsps. alkaline water
- 6 large grated zucchinis
- Sea salt
- 4 tbsps. ground Flax Seeds
- 2 tsps. olive oil
- 2 finely chopped jalapeño peppers
- 1/2 cup finely chopped scallions

Directions:

1. In a bowl, mix together water and the flax seeds then set it aside.
2. Pour oil in a large non-stick skillet then heat it on medium heat.
3. The add the black pepper, salt, and zucchini.
4. Cook for 3 minutes then transfer the zucchini into a large bowl.

5. Add the flax seed and the scallion's mixture then properly mix it.

6. Preheat a griddle then grease it lightly with the cooking spray.

7. Pour 1/4 of the zucchini mixture into griddle then cook for 3 minutes.

8. Flip the side carefully then cook for 2 more minutes.

9. Repeat the procedure with the remaining mixture in batches.

10. Serve.

Nutrition: Calories: 71 kcal Fat: 2.8g Carbs: 9.8g Protein: 3.7g

4. Hemp Seed Porridge

Preparation Time: 5 minutes

Cooking Time: 5 minutes

Servings: 6

Ingredients:

- 3 cups cooked hemp seed
- 1 packet Stevia
- 1 cup coconut milk

Directions:

1. In a saucepan, mix the rice and the coconut milk over moderate heat for about 5 minutes as you stir it constantly.

2. Reduce heat then add the Stevia. Stir.

3. Serve in 6 bowls.

4. Enjoy.

Nutrition: Calories: 236 kcal Fat: 1.8g Carbs: 48.3g Protein: 7g

LUNCH RECIPES

5. Almond Porridge

Preparation Time: 10 minutes

Cooking Time: 5 minutes

Servings: 1

Ingredients:

- Ground cloves, ¼ tsp.
- Nutmeg, ¼ tsp.
- Stevia, 1 tsp.
- Coconut cream, ¾ cup.
- Ground almonds, ½ cup.
- Ground cardamom, ¼ tsp.
- Ground cinnamon, 1 tsp.

Directions:

1. Set your pan over medium heat to cook the coconut cream for a few minutes
2. Stir in almonds and stevia to cook for 5 minutes
3. Mix in nutmeg, cardamom, and cinnamon

4. Enjoy while still hot

Nutrition: Calories: 695 Fat: 66.7 Fiber: 11.1 Carbs: 22 Protein: 14.3

6. Asparagus Frittata Recipe

Preparation Time: 20 minutes

Cooking Time: 20 minutes

Servings: 4

Ingredients:

- Bacon slices, chopped: 4

- Salt and black pepper

- Eggs (whisked): 8

- Asparagus (trimmed and chopped): 1 bunch

Directions:

1. Heat a pan, add bacon, stir and cook for 5 minutes.
2. Add asparagus, salt, and pepper, stir and cook for another 5 minutes.
3. Add the chilled eggs, spread them in the pan, let them stand in the oven and bake for 20 minutes at 350° F.
4. Share and divide between plates and serve for breakfast.

Nutrition: Calories: 251 carbs 16 Fat: 6 fiber 8 protein 7

7. Avocados Stuffed with Salmon

Preparation Time: 5 minutes

Cooking Time: 5 minutes

Servings: 2

Ingredients:

- Avocado (pitted and halved): 1
- Olive oil: 2 tablespoons
- Lemon juice: 1
- Smoked salmon (flaked): 2 ounces
- Goat cheese (crumbled): 1 ounce
- Salt and black pepper

Directions:

1. Combine the salmon with lemon juice, oil, cheese, salt, and pepper in your food processor and pulsate well.
2. Divide this mixture into avocado halves and serve.
3. Dish and Enjoy!

Nutrition: Calories: 300 Fat: 15 Fiber: 5 Carbs: 8 Protein: 16

8. Bacon and Brussels Sprout Breakfast

Preparation Time: 10 minutes

Cooking Time: 15 minutes

Servings: 3

Ingredients:

- Apple cider vinegar, 1½ tbsps.
- Salt
- Minced shallots, 2
- Minced garlic cloves, 2
- Medium eggs, 3
- Sliced Brussels sprouts, 12 oz.
- Black pepper
- Chopped bacon, 2 oz.
- Melted butter, 1 tbsp.

Directions:

1. Over medium heat, quick fry the bacon until crispy then reserve on a plate
2. Set the pan on fire again to fry garlic and shallots for 30 seconds

3. Stir in apple cider vinegar, Brussels sprouts, and seasoning to cook for five minutes

4. Add the bacon to cook for five minutes then stir in the butter and set a hole at the center

5. Crash the eggs to the pan and let cook fully

6. Enjoy

Nutrition: Calories: 275 Fat: 16.5 Fiber: 4.3 Carbs: 17.2 Protein: 17.4

DINNER RECIPES

9. Lasagna Spaghetti Squash

Preparation Time: 30 minutes

Cooking Time: 90 minutes

Servings: 6

Ingredients:

- 25 slices mozzarella cheese
- 1 large jar (40 oz.) Rao's Marinara sauce
- 30 oz. whole-milk ricotta cheese
- 2 large spaghetti squash, cooked (44 oz.)
- 4 lbs. ground beef

Directions:

1. Preheat your fryer to 375°F/190°C.
2. Slice the spaghetti squash and place it face down inside a fryer proof dish. Fill with water until covered.
3. Bake for 45 minutes until skin is soft.
4. Sear the meat until browned.

5. In a large skillet, heat the browned meat and marinara sauce. Set aside when warm.

6. Scrape the flesh off the cooked squash to resemble strands of spaghetti.

7. Layer the lasagna in a large greased pan in alternating layers of spaghetti squash, meat sauce, mozzarella, ricotta. Repeat until all increased have been used.

8. Bake for 30 minutes and serve!

Nutrition: Calories: 508 Carbs: 32 g Fat: 8 g Protein: 22 g Fiber: 21 g

10. Blue Cheese Chicken Wedges

Preparation Time: 20 minutes

Cooking Time: 45 minutes

Servings: 4

Ingredients:

- Blue cheese dressing
- 2 tbsp. crumbled blue cheese
- 4 strips of bacon
- 2 chicken breasts (boneless)
- 3/4 cup of your favorite buffalo sauce

Directions:

1. Boil a large pot of salted water.
2. Add in two chicken breasts to pot and cook for 28 minutes.
3. Turn off the heat and let the chicken rest for 10 minutes. Using a fork, pull the chicken apart into strips.
4. Cook and cool the bacon strips and put to the side.
5. On a medium heat, combine the chicken and buffalo sauce. Stir until hot.

6. Add the blue cheese and buffalo pulled chicken. Top with the cooked bacon crumble.

7. Serve and enjoy.

Nutrition: Calories: 309 Carbs: 27 g Fat: 18 g Protein: 34 g Fiber: 29 g

11. 'Oh so good' Salad

Preparation Time: 5 minutes

Cooking Time: 10 minutes

Servings: 2

Ingredients:

- 6 Brussels sprouts
- ½ tsp apple cider vinegar
- 1 tsp olive/grapeseed oil
- 1 grind of salt

- 1 tbsp. freshly grated parmesan

Directions:

1. Slice the clean Brussels sprouts in half.

2. Cut thin slices in the opposite direction.

3. Once sliced, cut the roots off and discard.

4. Toss together with the apple cider, oil and salt.

5. Sprinkle with the parmesan cheese, combine and enjoy!

Nutrition: Calories: 438 Carbs: 31 g Fat: 23 g Protein: 24 g Fiber: 16 g

12. Lemon Dill Trout

Preparation Time: 10 minutes

Cooking Time: 10 minutes

Servings: 1

Ingredients:

- 2 lb. pan-dressed trout (or other small fish), fresh or frozen
- 1 ½ tsp salt
- ½ cup butter or margarine
- 2 tbsp. dill weed
- 3 tbsp. lemon juice

Directions:

1. Cut the fish lengthwise and season the with pepper.
2. Prepare a skillet by melting the butter and dill weed.
3. Fry the fish on a high heat, flesh side down, for 2-3 minutes per side.
4. Remove the fish. Add the lemon juice to the butter and dill to create a sauce.
5. Serve the fish with the sauce.

Nutrition: Calories: 367 Carbs: 25 g Fat: 14 g Protein: 40 g Fiber: 21 g

VEG , LEAN & GREEN AND SALAD RECIPES

13. Mediterranean-Style Eggs with Spinach

Preparation Time: 3 minutes

Cooking Time: 12 minutes

Servings: 2

Ingredients:

- 2 tablespoons olive oil, melted

- 4 eggs, whisked

- 5 ounces' fresh spinach, chopped

- 1 medium-sized tomato, chopped

- 1 teaspoon fresh lemon juice

- 1/2 teaspoon coarse salt

- 1/2 teaspoon ground black pepper

- 1/2 cup of fresh basil, roughly chopped

Directions:

1. Add the olive oil to an Air Fryer baking pan. Make sure to tilt the pan to spread the oil evenly.

2. Simply combine the remaining ingredients, except for the basil leaves; whisk well until everything is well incorporated.

3. Cook in the preheated oven for 8 to 12 minutes at 280 degrees F. Garnish with fresh basil leaves. Serve.

Nutrition: Calories: 274 Fat,: 23.2g Carbs: 5.7g Protein: 13.7g Sugars: 2.6g Fiber: 2.6g

14. Spicy Zesty Broccoli with Tomato Sauce

Preparation Time: 5 minutes

Cooking Time: 15 minutes

Servings: 6

Ingredients:

- For the Broccoli Bites:
- 1 medium-sized head broccoli, broken into florets
- 1/2 teaspoon lemon zest, freshly grated
- 1/3 teaspoon fine sea salt
- 1/2 teaspoon hot paprika
- 1 teaspoon shallot powder
- 1 teaspoon porcini powder
- 1/2 teaspoon granulated garlic
- 1/3 teaspoon celery seeds
- 1 ½ tablespoons olive oil
- For the Hot Sauce:
- 1/2 cup tomato sauce
- 1 tablespoon balsamic vinegar
- ½ teaspoon ground allspice

Directions:

1. Toss all the ingredients for the broccoli bites in a mixing bowl, covering the broccoli florets on all sides.
2. Cook them in the preheated Air Fryer at 360 degrees for 13 to 15 minutes. In the meantime, mix all ingredients for the hot sauce.
3. Pause your Air Fryer, mix the broccoli with the prepared sauce and cook for a further 3 minutes. Bon appétit!

Nutrition: Calories: 70 Fat,: 3.8g Carbs: 5.8g Protein: 2g Sugars: 6.6g Fiber: 1.5g

15. <u>Broccoli with Herbs and Cheese</u>

Preparation Time: 8 minutes

Cooking Time: 17 minutes

Servings: 4

Ingredients:

- 1/3 cup grated yellow cheese
- 1 large-sized head broccoli, stemmed and cut small florets
- 2 1/2 tablespoons canola oil
- 2 teaspoons dried rosemary
- 2 teaspoons dried basil
- Salt and ground black pepper, to taste

Directions:

1. Bring a medium pan filled with a lightly salted water to a boil. Then, boil the broccoli florets for about 3 minutes.
2. Then, drain the broccoli florets well; toss them with the canola oil, rosemary, basil, salt and black pepper.
3. Set your oven to 390 degrees F; arrange the seasoned broccoli in the cooking basket; set the timer for 17

minutes. Toss the broccoli halfway through the cooking process.

4. Serve warm topped with grated cheese and enjoy!

Nutrition: Calories: 111 Fat,: 2.1g Carbs: 3.9g Protein: 8.9g Sugars: 1.2g Fiber: 0.4g

16. Family Favorite Stuffed Mushrooms

Preparation Time: 4 minutes

Cooking Time: 12 minutes

Servings: 2

Ingredients:

- 2 teaspoons cumin powder
- 4 garlic cloves, peeled and minced
- 1 small onion, peeled and chopped
- 18 medium-sized white mushrooms
- Fine sea salt and freshly ground black pepper, to your liking
- A pinch ground allspice
- 2 tablespoons olive oil

Directions:

1. First, clean the mushrooms; remove the middle stalks from the mushrooms to prepare the "shells".
2. Grab a mixing dish and thoroughly combine the remaining items. Fill the mushrooms with the prepared mixture.

3. Cook the mushrooms at 345 degrees F heat for 12 minutes. Enjoy!

Nutrition: Calories: 179 Fat,: 14.7g Carbs: 8.5g Protein: 5.5g Sugars: 4.6g Fiber: 2.6g

17. Famous Fried Pickles

Preparation Time: 5 minutes

Cooking Time: 15 minutes

Servings: 6

Ingredients:

- 1/3 cup milk
- 1 teaspoon garlic powder
- 2 medium-sized eggs
- 1 teaspoon fine sea salt
- 1/3 teaspoon chili powder
- 1/3 cup all-purpose flour
- 1/2 teaspoon shallot powder
- 2 jars sweet and sour pickle spears

Directions:

1. Pat the pickle spears dry with a kitchen towel. Then, take two mixing bowls.
2. Whisk the egg and milk in a bowl. In another bowl, combine all dry ingredients.

3. Firstly, dip the pickle spears into the dry mix; then coat each pickle with the egg/milk mixture; dredge them in the flour mixture again for additional coating.

4. Air fry battered pickles for 15 minutes at 385 degrees. Enjoy!

Nutrition: Calories: 58 Fat: 2g Carbs: 6.8g Protein: 3.2gSugars: 0.9g Fiber: 0.4g

18. Fried Squash Croquettes

Preparation Time: 5 minutes

Cooking Time: 17 minutes

Servings: 4

Ingredients:

- 1/3 cup all-purpose flour
- 1/3 teaspoon freshly ground black pepper, or more to taste
- 1/3 teaspoon dried sage
- 4 cloves garlic, minced
- 1 ½ tablespoons olive oil
- 1/3 butternut squash, peeled and grated
- 2 eggs, well whisked
- 1 teaspoon fine sea salt
- A pinch of ground allspice

Directions:

1. Thoroughly combine all ingredients in a mixing bowl.
2. Preheat your Air Fryer to 345 degrees and set the timer for 17 minutes; cook until your fritters are browned; serve right away.

Nutrition: Calories: 152 Fat,: 10.02g Carbs: 9.4g Protein: 5.8g Sugars: 0.3g Fiber: 0.4g

SEAFOOD

19. Nutritious Salmon

Preparation Time: 10 minutes

Cooking Time: 10 minutes

Servings: 2

Ingredients:

- 2 salmon fillets
- 1 tbsp. olive oil
- 1/4 tsp ground cardamom
- 1/2 tsp paprika
- Salt

Directions:

1. Preheat the air fryer to 350 F.
2. Coat salmon fillets with olive oil and season with paprika, cardamom, and salt and place into the air fryer basket.
3. Cook salmon for 10-12 minutes. Turn halfway through.
4. Serve and enjoy.

Nutrition: Calories: 160 Fat: 1 g Carbohydrates: 1 g Sugar 0.5 g Protein 22 g Cholesterol 60 mg

20. Shrimp Scampi

Preparation Time: 10 minutes

Cooking Time: 10 minutes

Servings: 4

Ingredients:

- 1 lb. shrimp, peeled and deveined
- 10 garlic cloves, peeled
- 2 tbsp. olive oil
- 1 fresh lemon, cut into wedges
- 1/4 cup parmesan cheese, grated
- 2 tbsp. butter, melted

Directions:

1. Preheat the air fryer to 370 F.
2. Mix together shrimp, lemon wedges, olive oil, and garlic cloves in a bowl.
3. Pour shrimp mixture into the air fryer pan and place into the air fryer and cook for 10 minutes.
4. Drizzle with melted butter and sprinkle with parmesan cheese.
5. Serve and enjoy.

Nutrition: Calories: 295 Fat,: 17 g Carbohydrates: 4 g Sugar 0.1 g Protein 29 g Cholesterol 260 mg

21. Lemon Chili Salmon

Preparation Time: 10 minutes

Cooking Time: 17 minutes

Servings: 4

Ingredients:

- 2 lbs. salmon fillet, skinless and boneless
- 2 lemon juice
- 1 orange juice
- 1 tbsp. olive oil
- 1 bunch fresh dill
- 1 chili, sliced
- Pepper
- Salt

Directions:

1. Preheat the air fryer to 325 F.
2. Place salmon fillets in air fryer baking pan and drizzle with olive oil, lemon juice, and orange juice.
3. Sprinkle chili slices over salmon and season with pepper and salt.
4. Place pan in the air fryer and cook for 15-17 minutes.

5. Garnish with dill and serve.

Nutrition: Calories: 339 Fat,: 17.5 g Carbohydrates: 2 g Sugar 2 g Protein 44 g Cholesterol 100 mg

22. Parmesan Walnut Salmon

Preparation Time: 10 minutes

Cooking Time: 12 minutes

Servings: 4

Ingredients:

- 4 salmon fillets
- 1/4 cup parmesan cheese, grated
- 1/2 cup walnuts
- 1 tsp olive oil
- 1 tbsp. lemon rind

Directions:

1. Preheat the air fryer to 370 F.
2. Spray an air fryer baking dish with cooking spray.
3. Place salmon on a baking dish.
4. Add walnuts into the food processor and process until finely ground.
5. Mix ground walnuts with parmesan cheese, oil, and lemon rind. Stir well.
6. Spoon walnut mixture over the salmon and press gently.

7. Place in the air fryer and cook for 12 minutes.

8. Serve and enjoy.

Nutrition: Calories: 420 Fat,: 27.4 g Carbohydrates: 2 g Sugar 0.3 g Protein 46.3 g Cholesterol 98 mg

SIDES ,SAUCES, SOUP & STEWS

23. Creamy Green Beans

Preparation Time: 10 minutes

Cooking Time: 15 minutes

Servings: 4

Ingredients:

- 1-pound green beans, trimmed
- 1 cup coconut cream
- 5 garlic cloves, minced
- A pinch of salt and black pepper
- 1 teaspoon sweet paprika

Directions:

1. In your instant pot, combine all the ingredients, put the lid on and cook on High for 15 minutes.
2. Release the pressure naturally for 10 minutes.
3. Divide the mix between plates and serve as a side dish.

Nutrition: Calories: 191 Fat: 7Fiber 4 Carbs 9 Protein 11

24. Cheesy Tomatoes

Preparation Time: 10 minutes

Cooking Time: 10 minutes

Servings: 4

Ingredients:

- 1-pound cherry tomatoes, halved
- ¼ cup veggie stock
- A pinch of cayenne pepper
- A pinch of salt and black pepper
- 1 tablespoon olive oil
- ¼ cup mozzarella, shredded

Directions:

1. In your instant pot, combine all the ingredients except the mozzarella, put the lid on and cook on High for 10 minutes.
2. Release the pressure naturally for 10 minutes, divide the mix between plates, sprinkle the mozzarella all over and serve.

Nutrition: Calories: 172 Fat: 4 Fiber 4 Carbs 9 Protein 8

25. <u>Beets and Pecans Mix</u>

Preparation Time: 10 minutes

Cooking Time: 20 minutes

Servings: 4

Ingredients:

- 2 cups water
- 1 red onion, sliced
- 4 beets
- 2 tablespoons olive oil
- 2 tablespoons balsamic vinegar
- A pinch of salt and black pepper
- 2 tablespoons pecans, chopped

Directions:

1. Add the water to your instant pot, add the steamer basket, add the beets inside, put the lid on and cook on High for 20 minutes.
2. Release the pressure naturally for 10 minutes, drain the beets, cool them down, peel and cut into cubes.
3. In a salad bowl, combine the beets with the rest of the ingredients, toss and serve as a side dish.

Nutrition: Calories: 142 Fat: 5 Fiber 3 Carbs 8 Protein 6

POULTRY AND MEAT

26. Apricot-Glazed Pork Chops

Preparation Time: 15 minutes

Cooking Time: 6 minutes

Servings: 6

Ingredients:

- 6 boneless pork chops
- ½ cup apricot preServings:
- 1 tablespoon balsamic vinegar
- 2 teaspoons olive oil
- Black pepper to taste

Directions:

1. Add oil to your cooker and heat on "chicken/meat," leaving the lid off.
2. Sprinkle black pepper on the pork chops.
3. Sear chops in the cooker on both sides till golden.
4. Mix balsamic and apricot preServings: together.
5. Pour over the pork and seal the cooker lid.

6. Adjust cook time to 6 minutes.

7. When time is up, hit "cancel" and quick-release.

8. Test temperature of pork - it should be 145-degrees F.

9. Rest for 5 minutes before serving!

Nutrition: Total Calories: 296 Protein: 20 Carbs: 18 Fat: 16 Fiber: 0

27. Easy Pork Ribs

Preparation Time: 10 minutes

Cooking Time: 15 minutes

Servings: 6

Ingredients:

- 3 pounds boneless pork ribs
- ½ cup soy sauce
- ¼ cup ketchup
- 2 tablespoons olive oil
- Black pepper to taste

Directions:

1. Pour oil into your PPCXL and hit "chicken/meat," leaving the lid off.
2. When oil is hot, add ribs and sear till golden on both sides.
3. In a bowl, mix black pepper, soy sauce, and ketchup.
4. Pour over ribs and seal the lid.
5. Adjust cook time to 15 minutes.
6. When the timer beeps, hit "cancel" and wait 5 minutes before quick-releasing.

7. Make sure pork is at least 145-degrees before serving.

Nutrition: Total Calories: 570 Protein: 65 Carbs: 0 Fat: 27 Fiber:

0

28. Pineapple-BBQ Pork

Preparation Time: 10 minutes

Cooking Time: 6 minutes

Servings: 4

Ingredients:

- 4 bone-in pork loin chops
- One 8-ounce can of undrained crushed pineapple
- 1 cup honey BBQ sauce
- 2 tablespoons chili sauce
- 1 tablespoon olive oil

Directions:

1. Mix can of pineapple, BBQ sauce, and chili sauce.
2. Turn your PPCXL to "chicken/meat" and heat.
3. When hot, add olive oil.
4. When the oil is sizzling, sear pork chops on both sides, 3-4 minutes per side.
5. When brown, pour sauce over the pork and seal the lid.
6. Adjust time to 6 minutes.
7. When time is up, hit "cancel" and wait 5 minutes before quick-releasing.

8. Pork should be cooked to 145-degrees.

9. Serve with sauce.

Nutrition: Total Calories: 370 Protein: 28 Carbs: 37 Fat: 13 Fiber: 0

29. Apple-Garlic Pork Loin

Preparation Time: 5 minutes

Cooking Time: 25 minutes

Servings: 12

Ingredients:

- One 3-pound boneless pork loin roast
- One 12-ounce jar of apple jelly
- 1/3 cup water
- 1 tablespoon Herbes de Provence
- 2 teaspoons minced garlic

Directions:

1. Put pork loin in your cooker. Cut in half if necessary.
2. Mix garlic, water, and jelly.
3. Pour over pork.
4. Season with Herbes de Provence.
5. Seal the lid.
6. Hit "chicken/meat" and adjust time to 25 minutes.
7. When time is up, hit "cancel" and wait 10 minutes before quick-releasing.

8. Pork should be served at 145-degrees. If not cooked through yet, hit "chicken/meat" and cook with the lid off until temperature is reached.

9. Rest for 15 minutes before slicing.

Nutrition: Total Calories: 236 Protein: 26 Carbs: 19 Fat: 6 Fiber: 0

OTHERS RECIPES

30. Pineapple Cornbread

Preparation Time: 10 minutes

Cooking Time: 15 minutes

Servings: 5

Ingredients:

- 1 (8½-oz.) package Jiffy corn muffin
- 7 oz. canned crushed pineapple
- 1/3 cup canned pineapple juice
- 1 egg

Directions:

1. In a bowl, mix together all the ingredients.
2. Place the mixture into the round cake pan.
3. Press "Power Button" of Air Fry Oven and turn the dial to select the "Air Fry" mode.
4. Set the cooking time to 15 minutes.
5. Now push the Temp button and rotate the dial to set the temperature at 330 degrees F.

6. Press "Start/Pause" button to start.

7. When the unit beeps to show that it is preheated, open the lid.

8. Arrange the pan in "Air Fry Basket" and insert in the oven.

9. Place the pan onto a wire rack for about 10-15 minutes.

10. Carefully, invert the bread onto a wire rack to cool completely before serving.

11. Cut the bread into desired-sized pieces and serve.

Nutrition: Calories: 222 Total Fat: 6.4 g Saturated Fat: 2.7 g Cholesterol 39 mg Sodium 424 mg Total Carbs 40 g Fiber 1.2 g Sugar 14.19 g Protein 3.8 g

31. Mini Rosemary Cornbread

Preparation Time: 15 minutes

Cooking Time: 25 minutes

Servings: 6

Ingredients:

- ¾ cup fine yellow cornmeal
- ½ cup sorghum flour
- ¼ cup tapioca starch
- ½ teaspoon xanthan gum
- 2 teaspoons baking powder
- ¼ cup granulated sugar
- ¼ teaspoon salt
- 1 cup plain almond milk
- 3 tablespoons olive oil
- 2 teaspoons fresh rosemary, minced

Directions:

1. In a large bowl, mix together the flour, cornmeal, starch, sugar, xanthan gum, baking powder, and salt.
2. Add the almond milk, oil, and rosemary. Mix until well combined.

3. Put the mixture into 4 greased ramekins evenly.

4. Press "Power Button" of Air Fry Oven and turn the dial to select the "Air Fry" mode.

5. Set the cooking time to 25 minutes.

6. Now push the Temp button and rotate the dial to set the temperature at 400 degrees F.

7. Press "Start/Pause" button to start.

8. When the unit beeps to show that it is preheated, open the lid.

9. Arrange the pan in "Air Fry Basket" and insert in the oven.

10. Place the ramekins onto a wire rack for about 10-15 minutes.

11. Carefully, invert the breads onto a wire rack to cool completely before serving.

Nutrition: Calories: 220 Total Fat: 8.5 g Saturated Fat: 1.1 g Cholesterol 0 mg Sodium 135 mg Total Carbs 35.5 g Fiber 2.8 g Sugar 8.6 g Protein 2.8 g

32. Monkey Bread

Preparation Time: 15 minutes

Cooking Time: 7 minutes

Servings: 8

Ingredients:

- 1 cup **Fat:**-free Greek yogurt
- 1 cup self-rising flour
- 1 teaspoon of sugar
- ½ teaspoon ground cinnamon
- 2 tablespoons butter, melted

Directions:

1. In a bowl, add the yogurt and flour and mix until a dough comes together.
2. Shape the dough into a ball.
3. Shape the dough ball into a flattened circle.
4. Cut the dough circle into 8 wedges and then, roll each into a ball.
5. In a plastic Ziploc bag, add the sugar, cinnamon and dough balls.
6. Seal the bag and shake well to coat evenly.

7. Arrange the dough balls in a greased loaf an.

8. Drizzle the dough balls with butter.

9. Press "Power Button" of Air Fry Oven and turn the dial to select the "Air Fry" mode.

10. Set the cooking time to 7 minutes.

11. Now push the Temp button and rotate the dial to set the temperature at 375 degrees F.

12. Press "Start/Pause" button to start.

13. When the unit beeps to show that it is preheated, open the lid.

14. Arrange the pan in "Air Fry Basket" and insert in the oven.

15. Place the pan onto a wire rack for about 5 minutes before serving.

Nutrition: Calories: 106 Total Fat: 3.4 g Saturated Fat: 2.2 g Cholesterol 9 mg Sodium 42 mg Total Carbs 14.7 g Fiber 0.5 g Sugar 2.7 g Protein 3.4 g

33. Apple Pull Apart bread

Preparation Time: 25 minutes

Cooking Time: 15 minutes

Servings: 4

Ingredients:

- 2 frozen dinner rolls, thawed overnight like Rhodes White Yeast Dinner Rolls
- 1 large Granny Smith apple, cored, peeled and chopped
- ¼ cup brown sugar
- ¼ cup granulated white sugar
- 4 teaspoons ground cinnamon, divided
- ¼ cup of unsalted butter, melted

Directions:

1. Cut the dinner rolls in half and then, flatten each into a 2-inch circle.
2. In a large bowl, add the apples, brown sugar and 2 teaspoons of cinnamon and mix well.
3. Place about 1 teaspoon of apple mixture filling in center of each circle.
4. Pinch the edges together to form a smooth ball.

5. Arrange the dough balls in the greased "Air Fry Basket" and insert in the oven. (Do not turn the oven on).

6. Let the dough rise for about 1 hour.

7. In a bowl, mix together the white sugar and remaining cinnamon.

8. Remove the basket from oven and brush the stuffed rolls with butter mixture generously.

9. Sprinkle with the cinnamon sugar on top.

10. Press "Power Button" of Air Fry Oven and turn the dial to select the "Air Fry" mode.

11. Press the Time button and again turn the dial to set the cooking time to 15 minutes.

12. Now push the Temp button and rotate the dial to set the temperature at 330 degrees F.

13. Press "Start/Pause" button to start.

14. When the unit beeps to show that it is preheated, open the lid.

15. Arrange the pan in "Air Fry Basket" and insert in the oven.

16. Place the pan onto a wire rack for about 5 minutes before serving.

Nutrition: Calories: 349 Total Fat: 14.4 g Saturated Fat: 7.9 g Cholesterol 32 mg Sodium 315 mg Total Carbs 52.8 g Fiber 3.4 g Sugar 29 g Protein 5 g

SNACKS AND APPETIZERS

34. Creamy Spinach and Shallots Dip

Preparation Time: 10 minutes

Cooking Time: 0 minutes

Servings: 4

Ingredients:

- 1 pound spinach, roughly chopped
- 2 shallots, chopped
- 2 tablespoons mint, chopped
- ¾ cup cream cheese, soft
- Salt and black pepper to the taste

Directions:

1. In a blender, combine the spinach with the shallots and the rest of the ingredients, and pulse well.
2. Divide into small bowls and serve as a party dip.

Nutrition: Calories: 204; Fat: 11.5 g; Fiber 3.1 g; Carbs 4.2 g; Protein 5.9 g

35. <u>Avocado Dip</u>

Preparation Time: 5 minutes

Cooking Time: 0 minutes

Servings: 8

Ingredients:

- ½ cup heavy cream
- 1 green chili pepper, chopped
- Salt and pepper to the taste
- 4 avocados, pitted, peeled and chopped
- 1 cup cilantro, chopped
- ¼ cup lime juice

Directions:

1. In a blender, combine the cream with the avocados and the rest of the ingredients and pulse well.
2. Divide the mix into bowls and serve cold as a party dip.

Nutrition: Calories: 200; Fat: 14.5 g; Fiber 3.8 g; Carbs 8.1 g; Protein 7.6 g

36. Goat Cheese and Chives Spread

Preparation Time: 10 minutes

Cooking Time: 0 minute

Servings: 4

Ingredients:

- 2 ounces goat cheese, crumbled
- ¾ cup sour cream
- 2 tablespoons chives, chopped
- 1 tablespoon lemon juice
- Salt and black pepper to the taste
- 2 tablespoons extra virgin olive oil

Directions:

1. In a bowl, mix the goat cheese with the cream and the rest of the ingredients and whisk really well.
2. Keep in the fridge for 10 minutes and serve as a party spread.

Nutrition: Calories: 220; Fat: 11.5 g; Fiber 4.8 g; Carbs 8.9 g; Protein 5.6 g

DESSERTS

37. Apple Couscous Pudding

Preparation Time: 10 minutes

Cooking Time: 25 minutes

Servings: 4

Ingredients:

- ½ cup couscous
- 1 and ½ cups milk
- ¼ cup apple, cored and chopped
- 3 tablespoons stevia
- ½ teaspoon rose water
- 1 tablespoon orange zest, grated

Directions:

1. Heat up a pan with the milk over medium heat,
2. add the couscous and the rest of the ingredients, whisk, simmer for 25 minutes, divide into bowls and serve.

Nutrition: Calories: 150 Fat: 4.5 Fiber 5.5 Carbs 7.5 Protein 4

38. Ricotta Ramekins

Preparation Time: 10 minutes

Cooking Time: 1 hour

Servings: 4

Ingredients:

- 6 eggs, whisked
- 1 and ½ pounds ricotta cheese, soft
- ½ pound stevia
- 1 teaspoon vanilla extract
- ½ teaspoon baking powder
- Cooking spray

Directions:

1. In a bowl, mix the eggs with the ricotta and the other ingredients except the cooking spray and whisk well.
2. Grease 4 ramekins with the cooking spray, pour the ricotta cream in each and bake at 360 degrees F for 1 hour.
3. Serve cold.

Nutrition: Calories: 180 Fat: 5.3 Fiber 5.4 Carbs 11.5 Protein 4

39. Papaya Cream

Preparation Time: 10 minutes

Cooking Time: 0 minutes

Servings: 2

Ingredients:

- 1 cup papaya, peeled and chopped
- 1 cup heavy cream
- 1 tablespoon stevia
- ½ teaspoon vanilla extract

Directions:

1. In a blender, combine the cream with the papaya and the other ingredients, pulse well, divide into cups and serve cold.

Nutrition: Calories: 182 Fat: 3.1 Fiber 2.3 Carbs 3.5 Protein 2

40. Strawberry Sorbet

Preparation Time: 15 minutes

Cooking Time: 10 minutes

Servings: 6

Ingredients:

- 1 cup strawberries, chopped
- 1 tablespoon of liquid honey

- 2 tablespoons water
- 1 tablespoon lemon juice

Directions:

1. Preheat the water and liquid honey until you get homogenous liquid.
2. Blend the strawberries until smooth and combine them with honey liquid and lemon juice.
3. Transfer the strawberry mixture in the ice cream maker and churn it for 20 minutes or until the sorbet is thick.
4. Scoop the cooked sorbet in the ice cream cups.

Nutrition: Calories: 30, Fat: 0.4 g, Fiber 1.4 g, Carbs 14.9 g, Protein 0.9 g

CPSIA information can be obtained
at www.ICGtesting.com
Printed in the USA
BVHW080942120521
607048BV00009B/2970